HUMAN REPRODUCTIVE BIOLOGY WORKBOOK

GIVON SANATI

Brainathlon Learning Systems

TABLE OF CONTENTS

CHAPTER 1.

ENDOCRINOLOGY

MATCHING

Section 1

Match each term with the appropriate definition.

1. Activin
2. Adenohypophysis
3. Agonists
4. Androgens
5. Antagonists
6. Cerebrospinal fluid
7. Corticotropin
8. Dopamine
9. Endocrine glands
10. Endocrinology

a. Enhances physiological response
b. Fluid that protects the brain
c. Inhibits physiological response
d. Neurotransmitter
e. Pituitary gland
f. Secretes ACTH
g. Secretes hormones into the blood
h. Study of endocrinology
i. Testosterone
j. Upregulates FSH

Section 2

Match each term with the appropriate definition.

1. Estrogens
2. Exocrine glands
3. Follicle-stimulating hormone
4. Gonadotropin-releasing hormone
5. Gonads
6. Hormone
7. Hypophysis
8. Hypothalamus
9. Inhibin
10. Melatonin

a. Chemical messenger
b. Circadian rhythm
c. Downregulates FSH
d. Female sex hormones
e. Mammary glands
f. Pituitary gland
g. Produces oxytocin and ADH
h. Released from the anterior pituitary gland
i. Stimulates the release at FSH and LH
j. Testes

Section 3

Match each term with the appropriate definition.

1. Luteinizing hormone
2. Negative feedback
3. Neurohormones
4. Neurohypophysis
5. Neurotransmitter
6. Norepinephrine
7. Oxytocin
8. Paracrines
9. Phytoestrogens
10. Pineal gland

a. An example is ADH
b. Dopamine
c. Estrogen derived from plants
d. Generates uterine contractions
e. Posterior pituitary
f. Released from the anterior pituitary gland
g. Secretes melatonin
h. Signaling to the neighboring cell
i. Stimulates a fight-or-flight response
j. Stimulus results in an inhibition of the response

Section 4

Match each term with the appropriate definition.

1. Polypeptides
2. Positive feedback
3. Progesterone
4. Prolactin
5. Steroid
6. Tamoxifen
7. Thyrotropin-releasing hormone
8. Thyroxine
9. Vasopressin
10. Xenoestrogens

a. An example is cortisol
b. Female sex hormones
c. Fluid retention
d. Protein
e. Regulates metabolism
f. Release of milk
g. Stimulate thyroid to release T3/T4
h. Stimulus results in an activation of the response
i. Synthetic estrogen
j. Treats breast cancer

MULTIPLE CHOICE

1. Which set of messengers acts on neighboring cells within the same tissue?
    a. Autocrines
    b. Paracrines
    c. Hormones
    d. None of the above

2. Which set of messengers acts on neighboring cells within the same tissue?
    a. Autocrines
    b. Paracrines
    c. Hormones
    d. None of the above

3. The main difference between hormones and neurotransmitters is that hormones reach their objective via _____.
    a. Target cell
    b. Blood
    c. Cerebrospinal fluid
    d. Ducts

4. A major determinant of a hormone's mechanism of action is _____.
    a. Physical property
    b. Size
    c. Rapid acting or slow acting
    d. Gene activation

5. Receptors for steroid hormones are located _____.
    a. In the blood plasma
    b. In the cytosol
    c. On the plasma membrane
    d. In the extracellular fluid

6. Interaction with a membrane-bound receptor will transduce the hormonal message via _____.
    a. Second messenger
    b. Repolarization
    c. Direct gene activation
    d. Endocytosis
    e. Exocytosis

7. To activate a target cell, a hormone must possess a _____.
    a. Second messenger
    b. Neurotransmitter
    c. Hormone
    d. Receptor

8. Which hormone is produced in the hypothalamus?
    a. Adrenocorticotropic hormone
    b. Anti-diuretic hormone
    c. Luteinizing hormone
    d. Growth hormone

9. Hormones secreted into the hypophyseal portal system are detected by the _____.
    a. Posterior pituitary
    b. Anterior pituitary
    c. Median eminence
    d. Infundibulum

10. Secretions from the corticotrophs activate cells of the _____, while secretions from the gonadotrophs affect cells of the _____.
    a. Thyroid; mammary glands
    b. Adrenal medulla; gonads
    c. Adrenal cortex; gonads
    d. Mammary glands; gonads

11. A patient is displaying polyuria, polydipsia and polyphagia. In addition to these symptoms, there is an instance of severe dehydration. The most likely cause is _____.
    a. Hypersecretion of ADH
    b. Hyposecretion of ADH
    c. Hypersecretion of oxytocin
    d. Hyposecretion of oxytocin

12. Sam is losing weight rapidly, sweating profusely, and experiences anxiety. Sam may be suffering from _____.
    a. Hypoparathyroidism
    b. Hyperparathyroidism
    c. Hyperthyroidism
    d. Hypothyroidism

13. Occasionally, Vanessa will experience hirsutism, or excessive facial hair growth. However, blood tests reveal that her levels of testosterone are normal for a female. Another explanation of this abnormality is caused by the hypersecretion of
    a. Gonadocorticoids
    b. Catecholamines
    c. Mineralocorticoids
    d. Glucocorticoids

14. What adrenal hormone responsible for maintaining appropriate blood sodium levels?
    a. Epinephrine
    b. Cortisol
    c. DHEA
    d. Aldosterone

15. _____ trigger(s) secretion of aldosterone.
    a. Angiotensin II
    b. Increased potassium
    c. ANP
    d. Increase sodium
    e. Both a and b

16. During test time, Tim experiences a high level of stress, where he became susceptible to a cold. This may be a result of elevated _____.
    a. Aldosterone
    b. Cortisol
    c. Androgens
    d. ACTH

17. Which of the following is not an action of glucagon?
    a. Release of glucose to the blood by liver cells
    b. Transport of glucose into cells
    c. Synthesis of glucose from lactic acid
    d. Breakdown of glycogen

18. What hormone helps regulate our circadian rhythms?
    a. Estrogen
    b. Melatonin
    c. Testosterone
    d. Thyroid hormones

19. This structure produces a hormone responsible for stimulating red blood cell production.
    a. Kidney
    b. Stomach
    c. Heart
    d. Skin

20. This structure produces a precursor to hormonal vitamin D, important for Ca2+ regulation.
    a. Stomach
    b. Skin
    c. Heart
    d. Brain

21. Endocrine glands differ from exocrine glands in that they do NOT have _____.
    a. Blood supply
    b. Chemical messengers
    c. Ducts
    d. Cells

22. Which of the following is NOT a hormone?
    a. Proteins
    b. Carbohydrates
    c. Eicosanoids
    d. Lipids

23. Target organs respond to water-soluble hormones because of the presence of _____ on the cell membrane surface.
    a. ATP
    b. Calcium
    c. cAMP
    d. Specific receptors

24. Most of the peptide hormones affect the target organs using _____.
    a. Intracellular receptors
    b. Intracellular second messengers
    c. Direct activation of genes
    d. Relay proteins

25. Hormones that directly activate genes are classified as _____.
    a. Water insoluble
    b. Water soluble
    c. Amino acid based
    d. G proteins

26. The islets of Langerhans are found in which endocrine organ?
    a. Thyroid gland
    b. Parathyroid gland
    c. Pancreas
    d. Adrenal gland

27. Oxytocin in produced in the _____.
    a. Ovary
    b. Hypothalamus
    c. Anterior pituitary gland
    d. Posterior pituitary gland

28. This hormone is involved in sodium regulation and therefore water balance.
    a. ADH
    b. Aldosterone
    c. Cortisol
    d. Glucagon
    e. DHEA

29. The target organ of thyrotropin-stimulating hormone is the _____.
    a. Posterior pituitary gland
    b. Anterior pituitary gland
    c. Thyroid gland
    d. Hypothalamus
    e. Thymus gland

30. _____ brain regulates the endocrine system.
    a. Hypothalamus
    b. Cerebral cortex
    c. Thalamus
    d. Neurohypophysis

31. The anterior pituitary stimulates other endocrine organs by secreting a group of hormones called _____.
    a. Releasing factors
    b. Tropic hormones
    c. Neurotransmitters
    d. Target hormones
    e. None of the above

32. Gigantism is a result of hypersecretion of this hormone.
    a. Growth hormone
    b. Thyroxine
    c. Cortisone
    d. Parathormone

33. Hypoglycemia is a result of a hypersecretion of which hormone?
    a. Glucagon
    b. Insulin
    c. Calcitonin
    d. Somatostatin

34. Cushing's disease is caused by _____.
    a. Hyposecretion of the adrenal cortex
    b. Hypersecretion of the adrenal cortex
    c. Hyposecretion of the pancreas
    d. Hypersecretion of the pancreas

35. Exophthalmos is a sign of hypersecretion of this hormone.
    a. Parathormone
    b. Thyroxine
    c. Calcitonin
    d. Growth hormone

FREE RESPONSE

1. There are various hormones released from various glands/groups of cells within the body. We discussed four different types of hormones in class. Differentiate between the types of chemical signaling below:

a. Endocrine

_____

_____

b. Paracrine

_____

_____

c. Autocrine

_____

_____

2. Give an example of the following types of hormones.

a. Proteins

_____

_____

b. Lipid

_____

_____

c. Amino Acid-Derived

_____

_____

3. List the cell types of the anterior pituitary that are targeted by the above hypothalamic hormones:

a. TRH:

_____

_____

b. CRH:

_____

_____

c. GnRH:

_____

_____

d. Dopamine:

_____

_____

e. GHRH:

_____

_____

4. How can a pituitary tumor lead to infertility if the gonadotrophs are intact?

_____
_____
_____
_____

5. If hormones secreted at the hypothalamus enter the capillaries, why are they not diluted when they arrive at the anterior pituitary?

_____
_____
_____
_____

6. What are the effects of GH?

_____
_____
_____
_____

7. It's Sam's 21st birthday. He's also extremely dehydrated. What problems may occur in this situation? Is this situation possible?

_____
_____
_____
_____

LABELING

Fig. 1.1

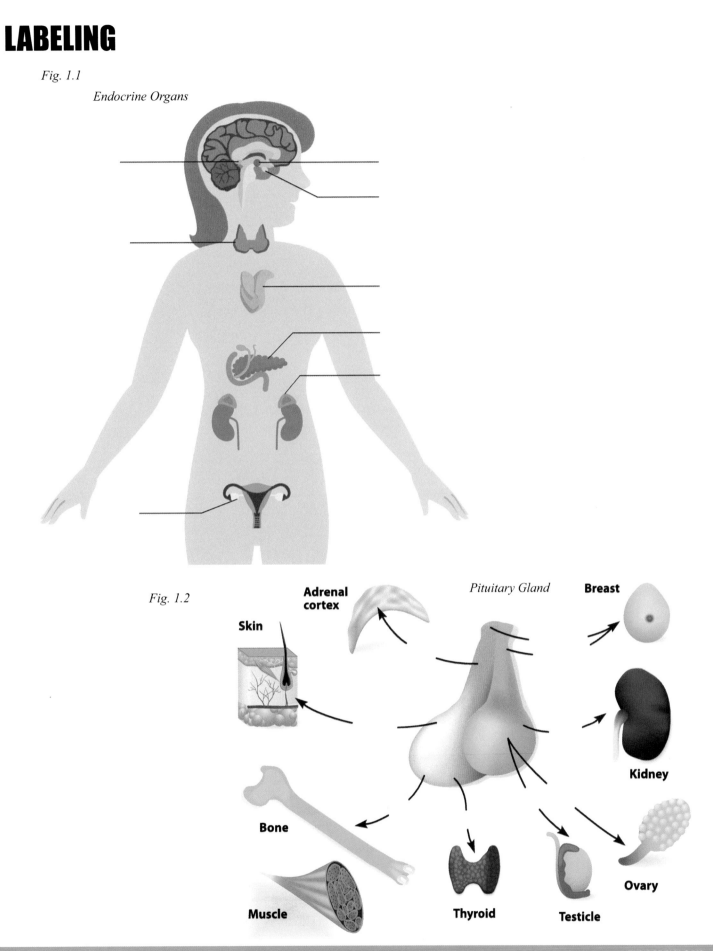

Endocrine Organs

Fig. 1.2

Adrenal cortex

Pituitary Gland

Breast

Skin

Kidney

Bone

Muscle

Thyroid

Testicle

Ovary

CHAPTER 2.

FEMALE REPRODUCTIVE SYSTEM

MATCHING

Section 1

Match each term with the appropriate definition.

1. Fallopian Tube
2. Uterus
3. Vagina
4. Cervix
5. Vulva
6. Breast
7. Ovum
8. Gonad
9. Ovary
10. Vestibular glands
11. Zona Pellucida
12. Mons Pubis
13. Lactiferous duct

a. Birth canal
b. Connect the nipple to the lobules of the mammary gland
c. Connects the ovary to the uterus
d. Contains the mammary glands for milk production
e. Female sex cell that unites with a male sperm to fertilized egg
f. Major female sex organs that produce eggs
g. Opening to the uterus
h. Organs that produces gametes
i. Secretes fluid for vaginal lubrication during coitus
j. Subcutaneous pad of adipose tissue covering the symphysis pubis
k. Surrounded oocyte after ovulation
l. The fleshy outer part of the female reproductive system
m. The womb

Section 2

Match each term with the appropriate definition.

1. Apoptosis
2. Aromatase
3. Cholesterol
4. Estrogen
5. Follicular atresia
6. Graafian follicles
7. Oogonium
8. Ovulation
9. Primary oocyte
10. Secondary oocyte
11. Testosterone

a. Degeneration of the ovarian follicle
b. Egg stem cell
c. Ejection of the ovum into the fallopian tub
d. Enzyme that converts testosterone to estrogen
e. Female sex hormone
f. Fluid-filled follicle that develops before ovulation
g. Lipid responsible for the production of steroids
h. Male sex hormone
i. Oocyte that is arrested in Metaphase II
j. Oocyte that is arrested in Prophase II
k. Programed cell death

Section 3

Match each term with the appropriate definition.

1. Cervical dysplasia
2. Endometrial polyp
3. Endometriosis
4. Fibroadenomas
5. Hysterectomy
6. Laparoscopy
7. Mastitis
8. Papanicolaou test
9. Pelvic inflammatory disease
10. Tamoxifen

a. Benign breast tumor
b. Benign growth attached to the endometrium
c. Cervical screening to detect abnormalities in the cervix
d. Chemotherapy for breast cancer
e. Development of abnormal cells in the cervix
f. Disease where uterine tissue grows outside of the uterus
g. Endoscopy through the abdominal walls
h. Inflammation of the breast tissue
i. Removal of the uterus
j. Results from urinary tract infection

MULTIPLE CHOICE

1. What is the superior portion of the uterus?
   a. Ampulla
   b. Fundus
   c. Infundibulum
   d. Isthmus
   e. None of the above

2. Which structure has fimbriae?
   a. Fallopian tube
   b. Uterus
   c. Ovary
   d. Vaginal canal
   e. None of the above

3. Follicular cells are part of the _____.
   a. Corpus albican
   b. Corpus luteum
   c. Primordial follicles
   d. Vesicular follicles
   e. None of the above

4. In a nursing mother, where does the milk accumulate?
   a. Areola
   b. Alveolar glands
   c. Lactiferous ducts
   d. Lactiferous sinuses
   e. None of the above

5. Which of the following is a secondary sexual characteristic promoted by estrogen?
   a. Enlargement of the external genitalia
   b. Development of the mammary glands
   c. Stimulation of oogenesis
   d. Thickening of cervical mucus
   e. None of the above

6. What hormone is responsible for milk ejection?
   a. Prolactin
   b. Oxytocin
   c. LH
   d. FSH
   e. None of the above

7. Which ligament anchors the uterus to the body wall?
   a. Broad ligament
   b. Perimetrium
   c. Round ligament
   d. Suspensory ligament
   e. None of the above

8. What is the areola part of?
   a. Testis
   b. Ovary
   c. Penis
   d. Breast
   e. None of the above

9. Which layer is the muscular layer of the uterus?
   a. Endometrium
   b. Myometrium
   c. Perimetrium
   d. Epimetrium
   e. None of the above

10. Which layer is the protective layer of the uterus?
    a. Endometrium
    b. Myometrium
    c. Perimetrium
    d. Epimetrium
    e. None of the above

11. What hormone is responsible for milk production?
    a. Prolactin
    b. Oxytocin
    c. LH
    d. FSH
    e. None of the above

12. Which layer of the uterus received the fertilized egg from the fallopoian tube?
    a. Endometrium
    b. Myometrium
    c. Perimetrium
    d. Epimetrium

13. Which of the following tissues of the female reproductive system contains erectile tissue?
    a. Vagina
    b. Clitoris
    c. Labia majora
    d. Cervix
    e. None of the above

14. Which of the following are risk factors for the development of breast cancer?
    a. Absent breast-feeding
    b. Early onset of menses
    c. Family history
    d. Late menopause
    e. All of the above

15. The infundibulum is not actually attached to the ovary and can allow pathogens to enter the abdominal cavity.
    a. True
    b. False

16. The fimbriae do not beat in a wave-like fashion but instead are stationary.
    a. True
    b. False

17. The outer serous layer of the uterine tube is part of the parietal peritoneum.
    a. True
    b. False

18. LH stimules the theca cells to secrete _____.
    a. Androgens
    b. Estrogen
    c. Progesterone
    d. Oocyte
    e. None of the above

19. What cell is responsible for the production of estrogen?
    a. Follicular
    b. Granulosa
    c. Oocytes
    d. Theca
    e. None of the above

20. A woman wants to get pregnant. She buys an "ovulation predictor" kit. Which of the following hormones would be the best indicator of ovulation?
    a. Estrogen
    b. Progesterone
    c. LH
    d. FSH
    e. GnRH

21. Which of the following is a secondary sexual characteristic promoted by estrogen?
    a. Growth of the mammary glands
    b. Enlargement of the external genitalia
    c. Stimulation of oogenesis
    d. Thickening of cervical mucus
    e. None of the above

22. Primary oocytes are produced during which process?
    a. Meiosis I
    b. Meiosis II
    c. Mitosis
    d. Oogenesis

23. Secondary oocytes are produced during which process?
    a. Meiosis I
    b. Meiosis II
    c. Mitosis
    d. Oogenesis

24. What are the follicular cells a part of?
    a. Tunica albuginea
    b. Corpus luteum
    c. Primordial follicles
    d. Vesicular follicles
    e. None of the above

25. Crossing over occurs during _____ .
    a. Anaphase II
    b. Prophase I
    c. Anaphase I
    d. Prophase I
    e. None of the above

26. The vagina has a low pH to prevent bacterial infections.
    a. True
    b. False

27. The Bartholin's glands are located on each side of the vaginal opening.
    a. True
    b. False

28. In males, gametes are formed by meiosis.
    a. True
    b. False

FREE RESPONSE

1. Describe the function of the female reproductive reproductive system.

_____

_____

_____

_____

2. List the important functions of granulosa cells and theca cells.

_____

_____

_____

_____

3. List the major functions of estrogen and progesterone.

_____

_____

_____

_____

4. Describe the Polycystic Ovarian Syndrome (PCO).

_____

_____

_____

_____

5. Name and define the type of glands in the female reproductive system.

_____

_____

_____

_____

6. What are the 3 layers of the uterus?

_____

_____

_____

_____

7. What are some female primary and secondary sex characteristics?

_____

_____

_____

_____

LABELING

Fig. 2.1

    Female Reproductive System

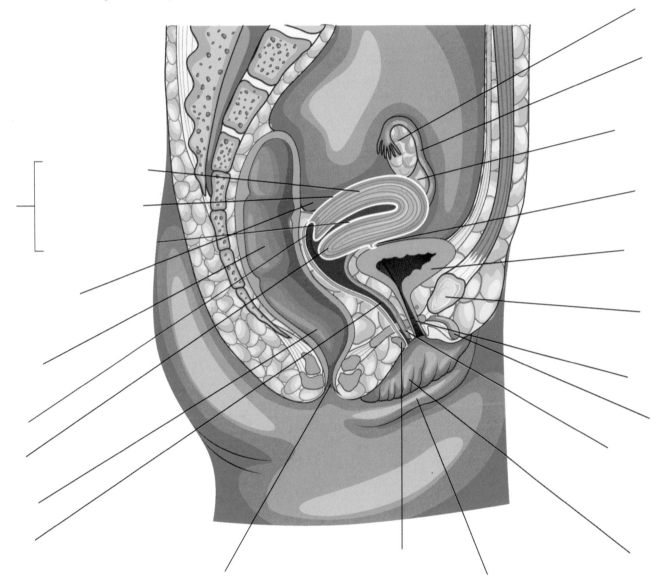

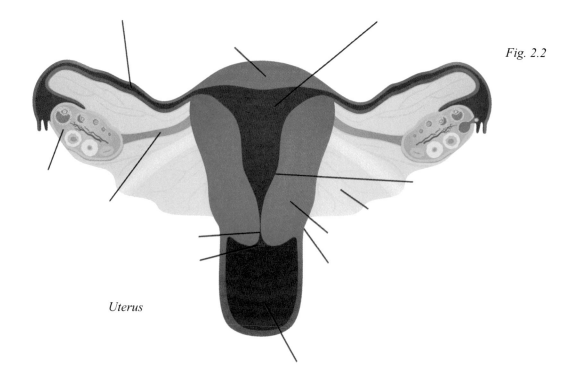

Fig. 2.2

Uterus

Fig. 2.3　*Breast Tissue*

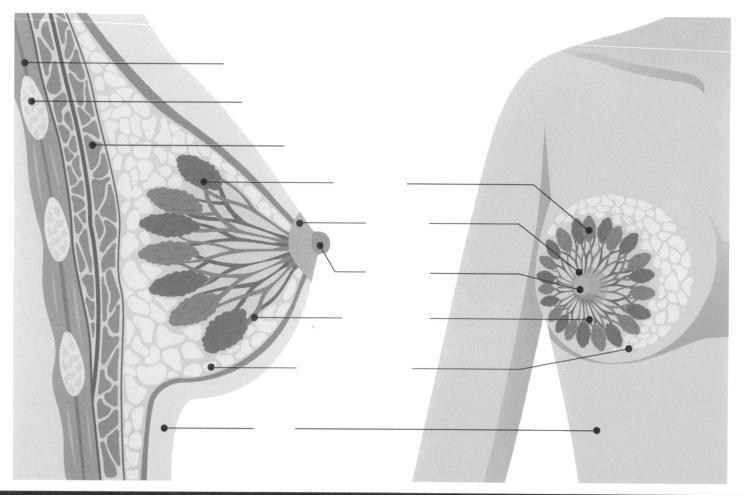

CHAPTER 3.

MENSTRUAL CYCLE

MATCHING

Section 1

Match each term with the appropriate definition.

1. Anestrous
2. Coitus
3. Edema
4. Follicular phase
5. Luteal phase
6. Menstruation
7. Mittelschmerz
8. Oophorectomy
9. Polyestrous

a. Alprazolam
b. Amenorrhea
c. Dysmenorrhea
d. Fern test
e. Fluoxetine
f. Oligomenorrhea
g. Pregnanediol
h. Premenstrual syndrome
i. Spinnbarheit

Section 2

Match each term with the appropriate definition.

1. Menorrhagia
2. Polymenorrhea
3. Intermenstrual
4. Hypermenorrhea
5. Oligomenorrhea
6. Hypomenorrhea

a. Abnormally heavy and prolonged menstruation
b. Abnormally heavy bleeding at menstruation.
c. Abnormally light and short menstruation
d. Cycle that occurs other than normal menstruation
e. Cycles with intervals of 21 days or fewer
f. Cycles with intervals of 35 days or greater

Section 3

Match each term with the appropriate definition.

1. Corpus albican
2. Dermoid cysts
3. Granulosa cell
4. Hirsutism
5. Ovarian cyst
6. Polycystic ovarian syndrome
7. Prostaglandin
8. Salpingitis
9. Taxol
10. Theca cell

a. Benign lump in the skin
b. Can lead to infertility in women
c. Chemotherapy for ovarian cancer
d. Degenerated corpus callosum
e. Excessive body hair
f. Fluid-filled sac within the ovary
g. Generates uterine contraction
h. Inflammation of the fallopian tube
i. Produces androgen in the female reproductive system
j. Produces estrogen in the female reproductive system

MULTIPLE CHOICE

1. What triggers ovulation?
   a. Prolactin
   b. Oxytocin
   c. LH
   d. FSH
   e. None of the above

2. Where does implantation of the fertilized egg usually take place?
   a. Ovary
   b. Oviduct
   c. Uterus
   d. Vagina
   e. None of the above

3. Where does fertilization typically occur?
   a. Fallopian tube
   b. Ovary
   c. Uterus
   d. Vagina
   e. None of the above

4. The ruptured follicle transforms into _____.
   a. Corpus albicans
   b. Corpus luteum
   c. Developing follicle
   d. Endometrium
   e. None of the above

5. How does the ovulated ovum enter the fallopian tube?
   a. Directly
   b. Diffusion
   c. Peristalsis
   d. Muscular contractions of the uterus
   e. None of the above

6. Prolactin supplementation will trigger a non-pregnant woman to _____.
   a. Initiate spontaneous pregnancy
   b. Mammary glands would begin lactation
   c. No change
   d. Vagina and uterus would necrose

7. Michelle wants to have kids with Hector. She buys an "ovulation predictor" kit. Which hormone does the kit monitor?
   a. Estrogen
   b. FSH
   c. Gnrh
   d. LH
   e. Progesterone

8. Luteal phase is the period before ovulation.
   a. True
   b. False

9. What does the ruptured follicle transform into after ovulation?
   a. Corpus luteum
   b. Antrum
   c. Uterine follicle
   d. Oviduct
   e. Corpus albican

10. The antrum is filled with fluid during the _____ phase.
    a. Follicular
    b. Luteal
    c. Proliferative
    d. Ovulation
    e. None of the above

11. FSH and LH are secreted by the posterior pituitary gland.
    a. True
    b. False

12. During the follicular phase, estrogen causes a surge of gonadotropins via positive feedback loop.
    a. True
    b. False

13. Immediately after ovulation, which structure secretes estrogen and progesterone?
    a. Primordial follicle
    b. Corpus albicans
    c. Corpus luteum
    d. Endometrium
    e. None of the above

14. During which phase of the uterine cycle is progesterone levels the highest?
    a. Menses
    b. Ovulation
    c. Proliferative phase
    d. Secretory phase

15. During the part of the normal menstrual cycle when the levels of progesterone and estrogen decrease, what will occur?
    a. Fertilization
    b. Menstruation
    c. Amenorrhea
    d. Ovulation

16. Which of the following is secreted by the corpus luteum?
    a. LH
    b. FSH
    c. GH
    d. Progesterone
    e. None of the above

17. Follicular phase is the period before ovulation.
    a. True
    b. False

18. Luteal phase is associated with an increase in progesterone levels.
    a. True
    b. False

FREE RESPONSE

1. What is the main trigger for the "LH Surge"?

_____
_____
_____
_____

2. What phase of replication are primary and secondary oocytes arrested?

_____
_____
_____
_____

3. Describe the follicular and luteal phase of the ovarian cycle.

_____
_____
_____
_____

4. What are some methods of detecting ovulation?

_____
_____
_____
_____

5. What are the symptoms of Premestrual Syndrome? List several treatment methods.

_____
_____
_____
_____

6. List and describe the phases of the uterine cycle.

_____
_____
_____
_____

Fig. 3.1

Ovary

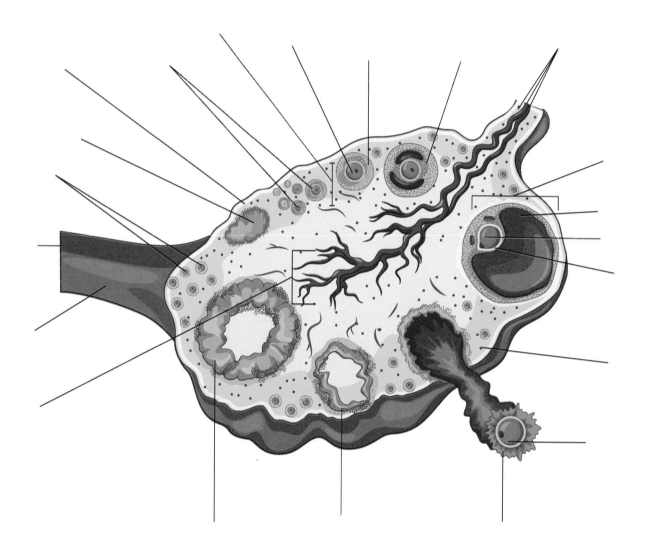

CHAPTER 4.

MALE REPRODUCTIVE SYSTEM

MATCHING

Section 1

Match each term with the appropriate definition.

1. Testes
2. Erection
3. Testosterone
4. Urethra
5. Seminal Vesicle
6. Ejaculation
7. Glans
8. Sperm
9. Scrotum
10. Semen

a. Fluid containing sperm
b. Gives sperm a shot of energy
c. Physiological phenomenon in which the penis is engorged with blood
d. Pouch of skin that protect the testicles
e. Primary sex organ in males
f. The head of the penis
g. The male gamete
h. The male sex hormone
i. The passageway through which urine and semen are released from the body
j. The release of semen from the body

Section 2

Match each term with the appropriate definition.

1. Area of the sperm cell gives motility
2. Area of the sperm cell that allows penetration of the egg
3. Area of the sperm cell that contains genetic information
4. Area of the sperm cell that contains many mitochondria
5. Crossovers
6. Homologous chromosomes separate from one another
7. Tetrads align along the cell's equator
8. Two haploid daughter cells are formed

a. Acrosome
b. Anaphase
c. Head
d. Metaphase
e. Neck
f. Prophase
g. Tail
h. Telophase

Section 3

Match each term with the appropriate definition.

1. Androgen binding protein
2. Bulbourethral gland
3. Cavernous urethra
4. Epididymis
5. Membranous urethra
6. Prostate gland
7. Prostatic urethra
8. Spermatogonia
9. Spermatozoa
10. Urethral orifice
11. Vas Deferens

a. Also known as the Cowper's gland
b. Duct that transports sperm from the testes to the urethra
c. Location of sperm maturation
d. Mature sperm
e. Opening of the urethra
f. Protein secreted by Sertoli cells that binds to testosterone
g. Region of the urethra that is contained in the corpus spongiosum
h. Releases prostatic fluid
i. Shortest and least dilated region of the urethra
j. Sperm stem cell
k. Widest and most dilated region of the urethra

Section 4

Match each term with the appropriate definition.

1. 5-alpha reductase
2. Benign prostatic hyperplasia
3. Cryptorchidism
4. Hypospadias
5. Libido
6. Orchidectomy
7. Primary spermatocyte
8. Prostate specific antigen
9. Secondary spermatocyte
10. Spermatid
11. Spermiation

a. Converts testosterone to DHT
b. Diploid cell
c. Enlargement of the prostate gland
d. Failure of the testes to descend
e. Haploid cell
f. Immature sperm cell
g. Lab test to detect for prostate cancer
h. Low sperm count
i. Maturation of sperm
j. Sex drive
k. Surgical removal of the testes

MULTIPLE CHOICE

1. What is the major difference between oogenesis and spermatogenesis?
   a. Oogenesis results in the formation of one viable oocyte.
   b. Oogenesis is the result of several mitotic divisions.
   c. Oogenesis is complete before ovulation occurs.
   d. None of the above

2. Primary spermatocytes are produced during which process?
   a. Meiosis I
   b. Meiosis II
   c. Mitosis
   d. Spermiogenesis

3. Tunica vaginalis is associated with the testes.
   a. True
   b. False

4. Secondary spermatocytes are produced during which process?
   a. Meiosis I
   b. Meiosis II
   c. Mitosis
   d. Spermiogenesis

5. Crossing over occurs during _____.
   a. Prophase II
   b. Metaphase II
   c. Prophase I
   d. Metaphase I

6. The testes are housed in the scrotum because they require lower temperature for proper development.
   a. True
   b. False

7. What would happen if someone developed an autoimmune disease in which the person's Sertoli cells were destroyed?
   a. Decrease in Testosterone levels
   b. Decrease in Estrogen levels
   c. Increase in Estrogen levels
   d. Increase in Testosterone levels

8. Which tissue is engorged with blood during the sexual arousal phase leading to an erection?
   a. Corpus spongiosum
   b. Corpora cavernosa
   c. Glans penis
   d. Prostate gland
   e. Testicles

9. Which region of the urethra runs through the penis and opens to the outside at the external urethral orifice?
   a. Membranous
   b. Penile
   c. Prostatic
   d. Spongy
   e. None of the above

10. What structure is responsible for producing seminal fluid?
    a. Testes
    b. Seminal vesicles
    c. Prostate gland
    d. B and C
    e. A and B
    f. None of the above

11. Seminal vesicle is located inferior to the urinary bladder.
    a. True
    b. False

12. During development of a male's brain, testosterone was not released. The gender identity may be ambiguous.
    a. True
    b. False

13. Tunica albuginea is associated with the testes.
    a. True
    b. False

14. As many as _____ sperm can be released with each ejaculation.
    a. 200
    b. 2000
    c. 600 million
    d. 600 trillion

15. _____ is a component in semen that stimulates the uterus to contract.
    a. Prostaglandins
    b. Fibrinogen
    c. Testosterone
    d. Estrogen
    e. LH

16. In males, Meiosis results in sperm formation. What is the critical step that will ensure proper chromosome number?
    a. Homologous chromosomes seperation
    b. Sister chromatids seperation
    c. Egg fertilization
    d. All of the above
    e. None of the above

17. Ductus deferens carries sperm from the scrotum to the abdominopelvic cavity.
    a. True
    b. False

18. Unlike females, males produce gametes throughout life. What is the reason for this phenomenon?
    a. Spermatozoa
    b. Spermatogonia
    c. Primary spermatocytes
    d. Secondary spermatocyte
    e. None of the above

19. Which of the following hormones do males secrete?
    a. Gnrh
    b. LH
    c. FSH
    d. Testosterone
    e. All of the above

20. Bulbo-urethral gland produces a thick, clear mucus.
    a. True
    b. False

21. During development of a male's brain, testosterone was not released. The brain might have a male orientation.
    a. True
    b. False

22. What percentage of sperm carry the Y chromosome?
    a. 20%
    b. 35%
    c. 50%
    d. 75%
    e. 100%

23. Epididymis carries sperm from the scrotum to the abdominopelvic cavity.
    a. True
    b. False

24. Pampiniform venous plexus is associated with the testes.
    a. True
    b. False

25. Bulbo-urethral is located inferior to the urinary bladder.
    a. True
    b. False

26. Primary spermatocytes are produced during mitosis.
    a. True
    b. False

27. Sperm is stored in the testes.
    a. True
    b. False

28. Sperm becomes mobile in the epididymus.
    a. True
    b. False

29. Which of the following hormones are required for spermatogenesis?
    a. GnRH
    b. FSH
    c. LH
    d. Testosterone
    e. All of the above

30. In males, gametes are formed by meiosis.
    a. True
    b. False

FREE RESPONSE

1. Describe the function of the male reproductive reproductive system.

_____
_____
_____
_____

2. List the important functions of Sertoli cells and Leydig cells

_____
_____
_____
_____

3. List the major functions of testosterone.

_____
_____
_____
_____

4. Which cells of the male reproductive system does follicular stimulating hormone and luteinizing hormone stimulate?

_____
_____
_____
_____

5. Describe the structure of a sperm.

_____
_____
_____
_____

6. What is the normal sperm count and volume ejaculate for a male?

_____
_____
_____
_____

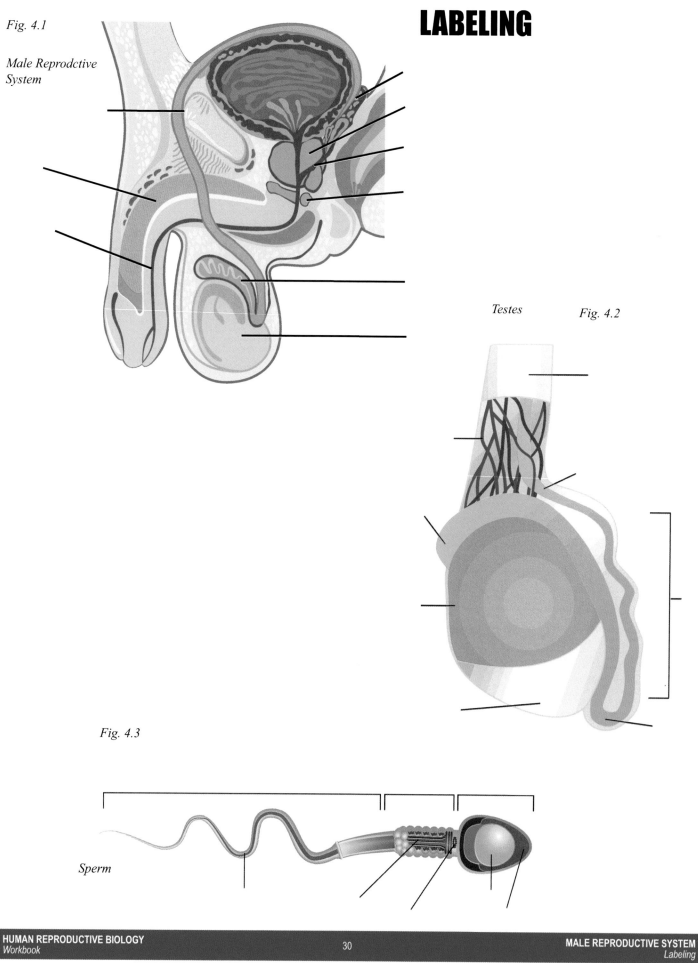

Fig. 4.1

Male Reprodctive
System

Testes   Fig. 4.2

Fig. 4.3

Sperm

CHAPTER 5.

SEXUAL DIFFERENTIATION

MATCHING

Section 1

Match each term with the appropriate definition.

1. Autosomes
2. Barr body
3. Duchenne's muscular dystrophy
4. Karyotype
5. Mullerian ducts
6. Sex chromosomes
7. Sex-determining region
8. Wolffian ducts
9. X linked

a. An X-linked recessive disorder
b. Chromosomes that determine the sex
c. Gives rise to the reproductive accessory structures in females
d. Gives rise to the reproductive accessory structures in males
e. Inactive X chromosome
f. Inheritances transmitted by the mother
g. Located on the Y chromosome
h. Non-sex chromosome
i. Used to detect chromosomal abnormalities

Section 2

Match each term with the appropriate definition.

1. Classical hemophilia
2. Dihydrotestosterone
3. Human chorionic gonadotropin
4. Intersexuality
5. Lesch-Nyhan syndrome
6. Mesonephric tubules
7. Müllerian-inhibiting factor
8. Testis-determining factor

a. Connects to the seminiferous tubule
b. Disorder where there is a lack in clotting factors
c. Inability to distinguish sex based on genotype or phenotype
d. Located on the Y chromosomes
e. Protein indicated conception via pregnancy test
f. Responsible for male secondary characteristic
g. Secreted by Sertoli cells
h. Symptoms include self-mutilation and gouty arthritis

Section 3

Match each term with the appropriate definition.

1. Androgen insensitivity syndrome
2. Congenital adrenal hyperplasia
3. Fragile-X syndrome
4. Gynandromorph
5. Klinefelter's syndrome
6. Nondisjunction
7. Penile agenesis
8. True hermaphrodite
9. Turner's syndrome

a. Abnormal chromosomal separation
b. Condition where both testicular and ovarian tissue is present
c. Congenital abnormality of the adrenal glands
d. Disorder diagnosed by behavioral and learning challenges
e. Genetically male that is born without a penis
f. Genetically male that is resistant to androgen
g. Organism that has both female and male characteristics
h. XO genotype
i. XXY genotype

MULTIPLE CHOICE

1. What are the sex chromosomes in females?
   a. XX
   b. XY
   c. XXX
   d. XXY

2. During early fetal development, the Mullerian duct gives rise to the female reproductive system.
   a. True
   b. False

3. Females with congenital adrenal hyperplasia demonstrate masculinisation of the external genitalia.
   a. True
   b. False

4. What are the sex chromosomes in males?
   a. XX
   b. XY
   c. XXX
   d. XXY

5. Which of the following structures have been concluded to be larger in female brain as compared with the male brain?
   a. Corpus callosum
   b. Hypothalamus
   c. Basal nuclei
   d. Pineal gland
   e. None of the above

6. During early fetal development, the Wolffian duct gives rise to the male reproductive system.
   a. True
   b. False

7. Hemophelia and color blindness is a Y-linked disease.
   a. True
   b. False

8. Which of the following structures have been concluded to be larger in male brain as compared with the female brain?
   a. Corpus callosum
   b. Hypothalamus
   c. Basal nuclei
   d. Pineal gland
   e. None of the above

9. Male sexual differentiation is a result of a default pathway due to the absence of the SRY gene.
   a. True
   b. False

10. The Y chromosome contains SRY gene that encodes the testis-determining factor
    a. True
    b. False

11. What is the sex chromosomes of patient with Turner Synderome?
    a. XX
    b. XY
    c. X
    d. XXY

12. A person diagnosed with psuedohermaphroditism present a combination of male and female gonadal tissues.
    a. True
    b. False

13. What are some congenital abnormalities that a patient with Turner syndrome display?
    a. Heart defects
    b. Short stature
    c. Webbed neck
    d. Infertility
    e. All of the above

14. Female embryo begins as a result of absent Anti-müllerian hormone and testosterone.
    a. True
    b. False

15. Intersex patients are born with an ambiguous reproductive system.
    a. True
    b. False

FREE RESPONSE

1. What is the role of MIS?

_____

_____

_____

_____

2. What is the role of SRY?

_____

_____

_____

_____

3. What is the androgen insensitivity syndrome?

_____

_____

_____

_____

4. What is the difference between true hermaphrodite and a pseudohermaphrodite?

_____

_____

_____

_____

5. How does the genital tract of a male fetus develop?

_____

_____

_____

_____

6. How does the genital tract of a female fetus develop?

_____

_____

_____

_____

CHAPTER 6.

MATCHING

Section 1

Match each term with the appropriate definition.

1. Puberty
2. Pubescence
3. Menarche
4. Sebaceous glands
5. Spontaneous erections
6. Nocturnal emissions
7. Tanner stages
8. Hydrocele

a. A period where individuals reach sexual maturity
b. Developmental scales in children, teens and adults
c. Fluid-filled sac around the testicle
d. Oil gland
e. Orgasm taking place during sleep
f. Penis becomes engorged with blood
g. Period where puberty begins
h. The beginning of menses

Section 2

Match each term with the appropriate definition.

1. Adolescence
2. Adrenarche
3. Gonadotropins
4. Gynecomastia
5. Inguinal hernia
6. Isotretinoin
7. Negative feedback
8. Positive feedback

a. Abnormal protrusion of tissue into the groin
b. An example is luteinizing hormone
c. Cessation of menses
d. Enlargement of breasts in men
e. Generic name is Accutane
f. Period subsequent to the onset of period
g. When the stimulus is present, response is activated
h. When the stimulus is present, response is inhibited

MULTIPLE CHOICE

1. At puberty, women experience menstruation.
   a. True
   b. False

2. What type of changes do teenagers experience during puberty?
   a. Physical
   b. Social
   c. Psychological
   d. Emotional
   e. All of the above

3. What physical changes do men NOT experience during puberty?
   a. Deeper voice
   b. Growth spurts
   c. Increase in size of penis and testes
   d. None of the above

4. What physical changes do women experience during puberty?
   a. Breast development
   b. Menstruation
   c. Developing wider hips
   d. All of the above

5. At puberty, menarche is characterized by the first menses in females.
   a. True
   b. False

6. Mood swings are closely related to the rapid increase in sex hormones.
   a. True
   b. False

7. Women secrete estrogen and progesterone during puberty to help promote the menstrual cycle.
   a. True
   b. False

8. All girls begin their menstrual cycle at the same time.
   a. True
   b. False

9. Men and women reach puberty at the same age.
   a. True
   b. False

10. What is the approximate age range of adolescence?
    a. 10 and 19
    b. 2 and 6
    c. 7 and 10
    d. 19 and 30
    e. none of the above

11. All individuals follow the same time and pattern of adolescence
    a. True
    b. False

12. What are the social changes that happen in puberty?
    a. Independence from parents
    b. Appearance becoming an important part of life
    c. Feelings of wanting to be accepted
    d. All of the above

13. All women are emotional before their periods.
    a. True
    b. False

14. Which male hormones increase during puberty?
    a. LH
    b. FSH
    c. Testosterone
    d. GH
    e. All of the above

15. _____ is a weak androgen from the adrenal glands, which marks the first endocrine change during puberty.
    a. Testosterone
    b. Estrogen
    c. Progesterone
    d. DHEA
    e. None of the above

16. Acne is a result of increased secretions of the skin's oil glands.
    a. True
    b. False

17. Which of the following factors DO NOT contribute to puberty?
    a. Social Interactions
    b. Nutrition
    c. Stress
    d. Climate
    e. None of the above

18. Nutritional deficiencies can contribute to irregular menses in women.
    a. True
    b. False

19. Family stress accelerates puberty in women.
    a. True
    b. False

20. At puberty, spermarche is characterized as the beginning of
    the development of sperm in males.
    a. True
    b. False

FREE RESPONSE

1. In females, describe the secondary sex characteristic that happens during puberty.

_____
_____
_____
_____

2. In males, describe the secondary sex characteristic that happens during puberty.

_____
_____
_____
_____

3. During puberty, what changes take place with hormones in males?

_____
_____
_____
_____

4. During puberty, what changes take place with hormones in females?

_____
_____
_____
_____

5. What are some factors that can alter the onset of puberty?

_____
_____
_____
_____

6. Describe some behavioral changes that take place during puberty.

_____
_____
_____
_____

CHAPTER 7.

REPRODUCTIVE
AGING

MATCHING

Section 1

Match each term with the appropriate definition.

1. Female climacteric
2. Hot flashes
3. Menopause
4. Perimenopause
5. Premature ovarian failure

a. Common symptom of menopause
b. Loss of ovarian function before the age of 40
c. Period of time before the onset of menopause
d. Permanent cessation of the menstrual cycle
e. Symptomatic menopausal state

Section 2

Match each term with the appropriate definition.

1. Androgen replacement therapy
2. Andropause
3. Estrogen replacement therapy
4. Human menopausal gonadotropin
5. Osteoporosis

a. Disorder where bones becomes brittle
b. Gradual decline of male sex hormone
c. Mixture of LH and FSH
d. Treatment for andropause
e. Treatment for menopause

MULTIPLE CHOICE

1. What hormones increase during Menopause?
   a. Estrogen
   b. Progesterone
   c. Luteinizing Hormone
   d. Two of the above
   e. All of the above

2. What age does menopause typically begin?
   a. 35
   b. 40
   c. 45
   d. 50
   e. 55

3. Menopause occurs in both males and females.
   a. True
   b. False

4. Which of the following are risk factors of HRT?
   a. Endometrial cancer
   b. Breast cancer
   c. Heart disease
   d. All of the above

5. Which of the following factors can cause premature menopause?
   a. Autoimmune disease
   b. Congenital
   c. Smoking
   d. Drinking
   e. All of the above

6. What percent of premenopausal women exhibit the symptoms of hot flashes?
   a. 25%
   b. 50%
   c. 75%
   d. 100%

7. Physician administers a blood test to confirm her patient's onset of menopause. Which of the following substance should increase to confirm the diagnosis?
   a. Cholesterol
   b. FSH
   c. Estrogen
   d. Progesterone
   e. None of the above

8. The most serious side effect of menopause is heart disease and osteoporosis.
   a. True
   b. False

9. Which of the following hormones is used to treat postmenopausal patients?
   a. LH
   b. FSH
   c. Estrogen
   d. Progesterone
   e. None of the above

10. Patient taking HRT may be at risk for certain cancers.
    a. True
    b. False

11. Natural estrogen is more potent that synthetic estrogen.
    a. True
    b. False

12. Patient experiences symptoms of osteoporosis. What does the doctor prescribe to prevent further progression?
    a. Calcium
    b. Vitamin D
    c. Calcitonin
    d. All of the above

13. Bone degeneration is a skeletal symptom of menopause.
    a. True
    b. False

14. Luteinizing hormone decreases after menopause.
    a. True
    b. False

15. What hormones decrease during Menopause?
    a. Estrogen
    b. Progesterone
    c. Luteinizing Hormone
    d. Two of the above
    e. All of the above

16. After menopause, the women's chances of pregnancy increase.
    a. True
    b. False

17. Estrogen replacement therapy is a type of HRT.
    a. True
    b. False

18. Which of the following symptoms are relieved with HRT?
    a. Hot flashes
    b. Night sweats
    c. Vaginal dryness
    d. Osteoporosis
    e. All of the above

19. Menopause occurs in women, whereas andropause occurs in men.
    a. True
    b. False

FREE RESPONSE

1. What are the signs and symptoms of menopause?

_____
_____
_____
_____

2. State the stages of the female reproductive cycle.

_____
_____
_____
_____

3. During menopause, what are the hormonal changes that take place?

_____
_____
_____
_____

4. Describe the treatment plan for osteoporosis.

_____
_____
_____
_____

5. Compare and contrast andropause with menopause.

_____
_____
_____
_____

6. What are the risk factors for hormone replacement therapy (HRT)?

_____
_____
_____
_____

CHAPTER 8.

THE HUMAN SEXUAL RESPONSE

MATCHING

Section 1

Match each term with the appropriate definition.

1. Androgyny
2. Erogenous zones
3. Erotic stimuli
4. Feminine
5. Gender identity
6. Masculine
7. Proceptive behavior
8. Sex role
9. Transsexuals

a. Area of the body that has heightened sensitivity
b. Attributes associated with females
c. Attributes associated with males
d. Behavior associated with a person's sex
e. Combination of masculine and feminine
f. Gender identity that is inconsistent with assigned gender
g. Individual feeling of one's own gender
h. Period in a relationship where courting takes place
i. Substance that triggers sexual arousal

Section 2

Match each term with the appropriate definition.

1. Arousal phase
2. Cremasteric reflex
3. Fellatio
4. Masturbation
5. Orgasmic phase
6. Plateau phase
7. Resolution
8. Sodomy

a. Associated with ejaculation in males
b. Females do not have this sexual response cycle
c. First stage of the sexual response cycle
d. Functions to ascend the testes
e. Oral sex
f. Phase of sexual arousal prior to orgasm
g. Sexual intercourse involving the anal cavity
h. Sexual stimulation of one's own genitals

MULTIPLE CHOICE

1. Vasocongestion is a process of muscle contractions and relaxations.
   a. True
   b. False

2. Which of the following stages of the sexual response cycle is absent in women?
   a. Orgasm
   b. Excitement
   c. Plateau
   d. Resolution
   e. None of the above

3. What phase of the sexual response cycle does a man experience an erection?
   a. Orgasm
   b. Excitement
   c. Plateau
   d. Resolution
   e. None of the above

4. What phase of the sexual response cycle does a woman experience vaginal lubrication?
   a. Orgasm
   b. Excitement
   c. Plateau
   d. Resolution
   e. None of the above

5. Vasocongestion is a process of blood accumulation in the genitals.
   a. True
   b. False

6. In the sexual response cycle, the refractory period occurs in males during the resolution stage.
   a. True
   b. False

7. During the arousal phase, how long until the onset of vaginal lubrication?
   a. Less than 30 seconds
   b. Between 30 to 60 seconds
   c. 60 to 120 seconds
   d. 1 hour
   e. None of the above

8. During the plateau phase, Cowper's gland secretes fluid at the tip of the penis.
   a. True
   b. False

9. Estrogen influences male sexual behavior.
   a. True
   b. False

10. Which of the following is false of a transsexual person?
    a. Man feels he is trapped in a women's body
    b. 40% suicide rate
    c. Experience severe clinical depression
    d. No clear evidence that sex change is effective
    e. All of the following are true

11. Which of the following can cause erectile dysfunction?
    a. Heart disease
    b. Depression
    c. Drugs
    d. Alcoholism
    e. All of the following

12. Ejaculatory incompetence is when the male ejaculates too soon.
    a. True
    b. False

13. Anti-hypertensive drugs are common medications used to treat sexual dysfunction.
    a. True
    b. False

FREE RESPONSE

1. List and describe the phases of the sexual response cycle.

_____
_____
_____
_____

2. What happens to the female reproductive organs during the sexual response cycle?

_____
_____
_____
_____

3. What happens to the male reproductive organs during the sexual response cycle?

_____
_____
_____
_____

4. What hormones influence sexual behavior in males and female?

_____
_____
_____
_____

5. List several causes of sexual dysfunction.

_____
_____
_____
_____

6. How is the sexual response cycle distinct when comparing males to females?

_____
_____
_____

CHAPTER 9.

GAMETE TRANSPORT
AND FERTILIZATION

MATCHING

Section 1

Match each term with the appropriate definition.

1. Acrosome
2. Cervical crypts
3. Coitus interruptus
4. Ejaculation
5. Fertilization
6. Hyaluronidase
7. Polyspermy
8. Thermotaxis

a. "Pull-out" method during sexual intercourse
b. Degrades hyaluronic acid
c. Fissures that secrete mucous in the cervix
d. Fusion of sperm and egg
e. Helps sperm penetrate the egg
f. Migration of cells via temperature
g. Releasing of seminal fluid
h. Two or more sperm fertilizing the egg

Section 2

Match each term with the appropriate definition.

1. Aneuploidy
2. Down syndrome
3. Fragile X syndrome
4. Fraternal twin
5. Identical twins
6. Parthenogenesis
7. Siamese twins
8. Triploidy
9. Ubiquitin

a. Also known as Trisomy 21
b. Born with an abnormal number of chromosomes
c. Born with an extra chromosome
d. Congenital disorder which causes intellectual disability
e. Conjoined twins
f. Development of an embryo from an unfertilized egg
g. Protein that marks for degradation
h. Twins that develope from same egg
i. Twins that develope from separate eggs

MULTIPLE CHOICE

1. The woman ovulates during the _____ day of the menstrual cycle.
   a. 1
   b. 4
   c. 10
   d. 14
   e. 20

2. After ovulation, the egg can be fertilized within _____ until it begins to degenerate.
   a. 6 hours
   b. 12 hours
   c. 18 hours
   d. 24 hours
   e. 48 hours
   f. 72 hours

3. To enhance the chances of conception, women should use douches with acidic solution.
   a. True
   b. False

4. During the first trimester, morning sickness is a typical problem.
   a. True
   b. False

5. How many sperm are in a typical ejaculate?
   a. 200
   b. 200,000
   c. 2 million
   d. 20 million
   e. 200 million

6. Which germ layer gives rise to the skin tissue?
   a. Endoderm
   b. Mesoderm
   c. Ectoderm
   d. Neural crest
   e. None of the above

7. Which germ layer gives rise to the muscular tissue?
   a. Endoderm
   b. Mesoderm
   c. Ectoderm
   d. Neural crest
   e. None of the above

8. Which germ layer gives rise to the gastrointestinal tissue?
   a. Endoderm
   b. Mesoderm
   c. Ectoderm
   d. Neural crest
   e. None of the above

9. Ectoderm cells will become the skeletal and muscular systems
   a. True
   b. False

10. Cell differentiation occurs when cells become specialized in structure and function.
    a. True
    b. False

11. Which of the following hormones cause the uterus to contract?
    a. Estrogen and Progesterone
    b. Oxytocin and Prostaglandin
    c. Prolactin and Progesterone
    d. FSH and LH

12. The fertilized egg undergoes cleavage forming a solid ball of cells of uniform size called _____.
    a. Zygote
    b. Morula
    c. Blastula
    d. Embryo
    e. Fetus

13. Which of the following hormones does the placenta NOT produce?
    a. Estrogen
    b. hCG
    c. Progesterone
    d. None of the above

14. How many days after fertilization takes place until the blastocysts develops?
    a. 1
    b. 2
    c. 3
    d. 4
    e. 5

15. The blastocyst is a combination of trophoblasts and embryoblasts.
    a. True
    b. False

16. The primordial germ cells create the yolk sac.
    a. True
    b. False

17. What determines the sex of the baby?
    a. Paternal gametes
    b. Maternal gametes
    c. Mom's emotion
    d. Embryo's emotion
    e. None of the above

18. What is the proper term for a fertilized egg?
    a. Haploid
    b. Diploid
    c. Ovum
    d. Zygote
    e. Blastocyst

19. Implantation is the attachment of the zygote to the uterus.
    a. True
    b. False

20. The percentage of a couple to have a female child is _____.
    a. 25
    b. 50
    c. 75
    d. 100

21. Another name for the "virgin birth" is called parthenogenesis.
    a. True
    b. False

22. Which of the following conditions below is characterized by a XXY genotype?
    a. Down Syndrome
    b. Turner Syndrome
    c. Kleinfelder's Syndrome
    d. None of the above

23. Non-disjunction is characterized by an abnormal separation of chromosomes.
    a. True
    b. False

24. Fraternal twins occurs when the early embryo splits into two separate organisms.
    a. True
    b. False

FREE RESPONSE

1. What substance is composed in semen?

_____
_____
_____
_____

2. Describe the process of sperm capacitation and activation.

_____
_____
_____
_____

3. List the stages of fertilization.

_____
_____
_____
_____

4. What is parthenogenesis?

_____
_____
_____
_____

5. Compare and contrast the two different types of twins.

_____
_____
_____
_____

6. Describe the pathway that sperm must migrate to transmit its genetic information.

_____
_____
_____
_____

7. How does the ovum prevent a multiple sperm fertilization?

_____
_____
_____
_____

LABELING

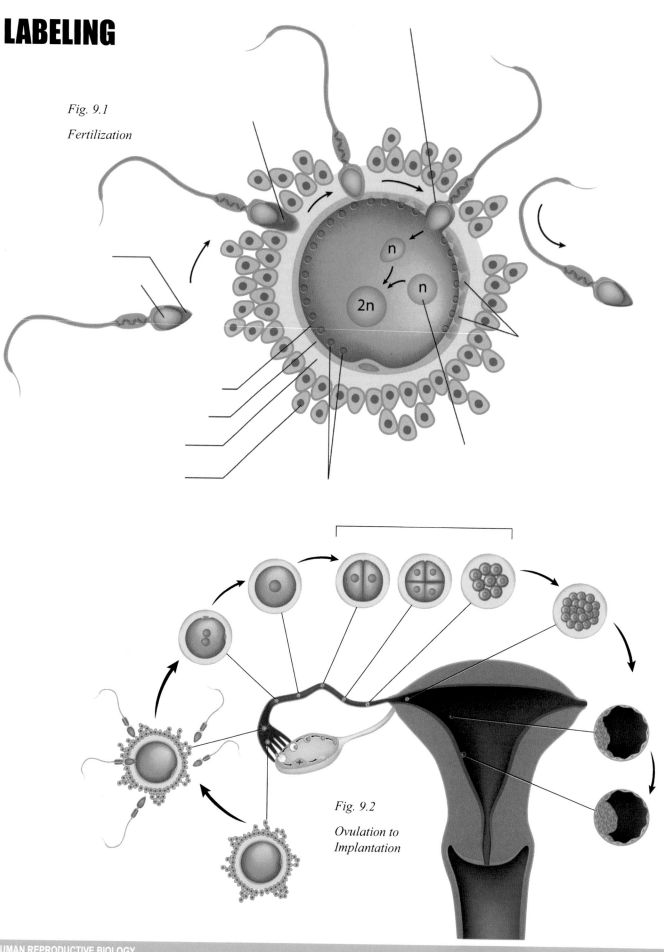

Fig. 9.1

Fertilization

Fig. 9.2

Ovulation to
Implantation

CHAPTER 10.

PREGNANCY AND LABOR

MATCHING

Section 1

Match each term with the appropriate definition.

1. Ectodermal layer
2. Endodermal layer
3. Epiblast
4. hCG
5. Hypoblast
6. Mesodermal layer
7. Morula
8. Pseudocyesis
9. Zona pellucida
10. Zygote

a. 16-cell after fertilization
b. False pregnancy
c. Fertilized egg
d. Innermost layer of the embryo
e. Layer that gives rise to digestive tissue
f. Layer that gives rise to muscular tissue
g. Layer that gives rise to nervous tissue
h. Outermost layer of the embryo
i. Protein that is identified in pregnancy tests
j. Surrounds the egg before implantation

Section 2

Match each term with the appropriate definition.

1. Amnion
2. Chorion
3. Ductus arteriosus
4. Ductus venosus
5. Foramen ovale
6. Meconium
7. Pitocin
8. Umbilical artery
9. Umbilical cord
10. Umbilical vein
11. Yolk sac

a. Connect the pulmonary artery to the aorta
b. Contains deoxygenated blood
c. Contains oxygenated blood
d. Contains the arteries and veins of the fetus
e. Encloses the embryo
f. Feces of a newborn infant
g. Permits oxygenated blood from right to left atria
h. Permits oxygenated blood to evade the liver
i. Plays a role in the formation of the placenta
j. Provides nourishment for the embryo
k. Synthetic oxytocin

Section 3

Match each term with the appropriate definition.

1. Cerebral palsy
2. Ectromelia
3. Ferguson reflex
4. Hydatidiform moles
5. Jaundice
6. Minimata's disease
7. Miscarriage
8. Mutagen
9. Parturition
10. Placenta previa
11. Stillbirth

a. Benign tumor that arises from a nonviable pregnancy
b. Birth of an infant that has died in the womb
c. Born with absent or defective long bone
d. Fetal ejection reflex
e. Genetic disorder of movement and muscle tone
f. Labor and delivery
g. Placenta covers the mother's cervix
h. Results from severe mercury poisoning
i. Spontaneous loss of a woman's pregnancy
j. Substance that causes mutation
k. Yellowing of the skin due to abnormal amount of bilirubin

Section 4

Match each term with the appropriate definition.

1. Anesthetics
2. Braxton Hicks contraction
3. Cervical effacement
4. Cesarean delivery
5. Episiotomy
6. Forceps delivery
7. Hematopoietic stem cell
8. Induce labor
9. Perineum
10. Superfetation

a. Area between the vulva and the anus
b. Assisted vaginal delivery using an instrument
c. Cell that gives rise to blood cells
d. Delivery of the baby through the abdomen
e. False contractions
f. Prostaglandin is administered for this procedure
g. Substance that induces numbing
h. Surgical incision of the perineum
i. Thinning of the cervix
j. Two fertilizations that take place at different times

MULTIPLE CHOICE

1. A Caesarean section may be required if the patient's cervix is not dilating
   a. True
   b. False

2. The cervix must dilate to _____ cm before a baby can be born.
   a. 1
   b. 5
   c. 10
   d. 15
   e. 20

3. Amniocentesis and Chorionic villi sampling are useful techniques for genetic screening.
   a. True
   b. False

4. Cocaine abuse during pregnancy can be related to a baby with low birth weight and mental retardation.
   a. True
   b. False

5. A Caesarean section may be required if the patient is diagnosed with Rh incompatibility.
   a. True
   b. False

6. Braxton-Hicks refers to:
   a. Blood pregnancy test
   b. Calculation of expected delivery date
   c. Contractions
   d. Urine pregnancy test
   e. None of the above

7. Pregnant women should avoid smoking and drinking to prevent any defects to their baby.
   a. True
   b. False

8. Genetic counseling is a procedure used to monitor genetic mutation before a baby is born.
   a. True
   b. False

9. Low birth weight is due to a mother having multiple births.
   a. True
   b. False

10. Which of the following is NOT part of the birth process?
    a. Cervical dilation
    b. Release of the embryo
    c. Release of the fetus
    d. Release of the placenta
    e. None of the above

11. What percent of the births demonstrate a breech presentation?
    a. 1
    b. 3
    c. 7
    d. 10
    e. 20

12. Which of the following medication is administered to induce labor?
    a. Estrogen
    b. Testosterone
    c. Oxytocin
    d. Progesterone
    e. None of the above

FREE RESPONSE

1. What are the signs and symptoms of pregnancy?

_____
_____
_____
_____

2. Explain the mechanism of the pregnancy test.

_____
_____
_____
_____

3. Describe the process of implantation.

_____
_____
_____
_____

4. What happens during embryogenesis?

_____
_____
_____
_____

5. During fetal development, how does the baby receive nutrients?

_____
_____
_____
_____

6. List several fetal disorders that result from exposure to mutagens.

_____
_____
_____
_____

7. What are some environmental factors that can cause genetic mutations?

_____
_____
_____
_____

8. What are the hormonal initiation that results in birth?

_____
_____
_____
_____

9. A pregnant patient walks into the hospital. She has passed her due date. Her physician is going to administer drugs to induce labor. What are the drugs and their respective functions?

_____
_____
_____
_____

10. Describe the steps in the birth process.

_____
_____
_____
_____

11. What are premature births? List some causes of their occurrences.

_____
_____
_____
_____

12. List and define the types of fetal positions.

_____
_____
_____
_____

13. What are the different types of deliveries?

_____
_____
_____
_____

CHAPTER 11.

BABY BLOCKERS

MATCHING

Section 1

Match each term with the appropriate definition.

1. Cervical cap
2. Combination pill
3. Condom
4. Contraception
5. Depo-Provera
6. Intrauterine device
7. Minipill
8. Spermicide
9. Tubal ligation
10. Vasectomy

a. "The Shot"
b. Chemical that kills sperm
c. Contains estrogen and progestin
d. Contains progestin only
e. Female barrier contraceptive method
f. Male barrier contraceptive method
g. Method to prevent conception
h. Surgical removal of the fallopian tube
i. Surgical removal of vas deferens
j. T-shaped piece of plastic inserted in the uterus

Section 2

Match each term with the appropriate definition.

1. Colpotomy
2. Culdoscopy
3. Dalkon shield
4. Endometritis
5. Hysterosalpingogram
6. Laparotomy
7. Plan B
8. Vaginitis
9. Xulane

a. Contraceptive intrauterine device
b. Contraceptive patch
c. Emergency contraceptive pill
d. Endoscopy of the rectouterine pouch
e. Inflammation of the inner lining of the uterus
f. Inflammation of the vaginal canal
g. Surgical incision in the back wall of the vagina
h. Surgical procedure to observe abdominal cavity
i. Visualization of the uterus and fallopian tube

Section 3

Match each term with the appropriate definition.

1. D&C
2. D&E
3. D&X
4. Essure
5. Hysterectomy
6. Induced abortion
7. Methotrexate
8. Mifepristone
9. Vacuum aspiration

a. Chemotherapeutic and immunosuppressive drug
b. Dilation and curettage of the endometrial lining
c. Dilation and evacuation of the endometrial lining
d. Dilation and extraction of the endometrial lining
e. Ending of a pregnancy due to the removal of embryo or fetus
f. Medication to induce an abortion
g. Procedure that induces fibrosis of the oviduct
h. Surgical removal of the uterus
i. Technique used to remove content from the uterus via the cervix

MULTIPLE CHOICE

1. What is inhibited after female sterilization?
   a. Ovum
   b. Estrogen
   c. Progesterone
   d. Testosterone
   e. None of the above

2. Before advising a 29-year-old client desiring oral contraceptives for family planning, the nurse would assess the client for signs and symptoms of which of the following?
   a. Acne
   b. Anemia
   c. Hypertension
   d. Influenza
   e. None of the above

3. Which of the following contraceptives is irreversible?
   a. Vasectomy
   b. Spermicide
   c. Diaphragm
   d. Plan B
   e. None of the above

4. Which of the following is the most effective contraceptive procedure?
   a. Spermicide
   b. Diaphragm
   c. Abstinence
   d. Plan B
   e. None of the above

5. What are some common problems associated with tubal ligations?
   a. Increase in depression
   b. Increase in libido
   c. Increase in vaginal sensitivity
   d. None of the above

6. Which type of contraceptive decreases sperm mobility and is required with female barrier methods?
   a. Condom
   b. Spermicide
   c. Diaphragm
   d. Plan B
   e. None of the above

7. Spermicides may generate an allergic reaction.
   a. True
   b. False

8. What are some advantages of male condoms?
   a. Inexpensive
   b. Prevents pregnancy
   c. Prevents the transmission of STI's
   d. No prescriptions
   e. All of the above

9. One of the disadvantages of male condoms is that it promotes less penile sensation in some men.
   a. True
   b. False

10. This is a lubricated vaginal sheath and it is anchored around the cervix and covers the labia.
    a. Plan B
    b. Condom
    c. IUD
    d. Cervical cap
    e. None of the above

11. The advantage of a women using a diaphragm is that there are no hormonal alterations.
    a. True
    b. False

12. Hormonal contraceptive methods work to suppress the action of the hypothalamus and anterior pituitary.
    a. True
    b. False

13. Tubal ligation _____.
    a. Inhibit estrogen production
    b. Inhibit progesterone production
    c. Interferes with vaginal lubrication
    d. Decreases egg count
    e. None of the above

14. Which hormone(s) do birth control pills inhibit?
    a. FSH
    b. Estrogen
    c. LH
    d. Two of the above
    e. All of the above

15. Which type of contraceptive uses a T-shaped piece of flexible plastic that is placed in the uterus?
    a. Contraceptive patch
    b. Emergency contraceptive
    c. IUD
    d. Injectable progestogen
    e. None of the above

16. Breast feeding is the body's natural contraceptive.
    a. True
    b. False

17. What are the absolute contradictions for hormonal methods?
    a. Cancer
    b. Thrombosis
    c. Cardiovascular disease
    d. Alzheimer's disease
    e. All of the above

18. Women must begin taking their birth control pill on day 11 of the menstrual cycle.
    a. True
    b. False

19. Combination pill is associated with breast cancer.
    a. True
    b. False

20. Which of the following disorders are associated with IUDs?
    a. PID
    b. Tubal infection
    c. Uterine infection
    d. Fallopian infection
    e. All of the above

21. Which of the following side effects has been associated with use of the condom?
    a. Infections
    b. Abdominal pain
    c. Hypertension
    d. Cancer
    e. None of the above

22. Vasectomies cause a _____.
    a. Increase in testosterone
    b. Increase in the rigidity of the penis
    c. Increase in sperm production
    d. Decrease in organism
    e. None of the above

FREE RESPONSE

1. What is the purpose of contraceptives?

_____
_____
_____
_____

2. What is Plan B?

_____
_____
_____
_____

3. How do birth control pills work? What are the possible side effects?

_____
_____
_____
_____

4. List and describe some male contraceptives.

_____
_____
_____
_____

5. What are the surgical contraceptives for males and females?

_____
_____
_____
_____

6. What are the pros and cons of condoms?

_____
_____
_____
_____

7. Why is it recommended to not use spermicides?

_____
_____
_____
_____

8. What are the various surgical techniques used to induce abortions?

_____

_____

_____

_____

_____

9. What are the consequences of induced abortions?

_____

_____

_____

_____

_____

CHAPTER 12.

INFERTILITY

MATCHING

Section 1

Match each term with the appropriate definition.

1. Azoospermia
2. Bromocriptine
3. Clomiphene
4. Huhner's test
5. Infertility
6. Oligospermia
7. Pergonal
8. Retrograde ejaculation
9. Testicular biopsy
10. Varicocele

a. Absence of sperm from semen
b. Dilation of veins within the scrotum
c. Dopamine agonist
d. Drug that treats infertility in women
e. Entry of semen into the bladder rather than urethra
f. Evaluate for testicular cancer
g. Examination for infertility
h. Inability to produce offspring
i. Low sperm count
j. Mixture of gonadotropin hormones for infertility

Section 2

Match each term with the appropriate definition.

1. Adoption
2. Assisted hatching
3. Cloning
4. Cytoplasmic transfer
5. GIFT
6. Impotence
7. In vitro fertilization
8. Intracytoplasmic sperm injection
9. ZIFT

a. Create an identical copy
b. Gamete intrafallopian transfer
c. Man's inability to achieve an erection
d. Person accepts the parenting role of another's child
e. Sperm and egg fuse outside of the body
f. Sperm cell is directly injected into the cytoplasm of the egg
g. Transfer of cell organelles from donor egg to recipient egg
h. Zona drilling
i. Zygote intrafallopian transfer

MULTIPLE CHOICE

1. Cat and Richard have been trying to have a baby for over a year. They found out that Cat's ovum was viable even after the harsh IUDs she regrettably placed to prevent pregnancy. What fertility method would be the primary candidate?
   a. Adoption
   b. In vitro fertilization
   c. Artificial insemination
   d. Embryonic transfer
   e. None of the above

2. Declining steroid hormones (estrogen and progesterone) may cause infertility in females.
   a. True
   b. False

3. Patient diagnosed with endometriosis may exhibits signs of infertility.
   a. True
   b. False

4. Where does fertilization normally occur?
   a. Vagina
   b. Oviduct
   c. Ovary
   d. Cervix
   e. None of the above

5. Engaging in coitus within a few hours of ovulation enhances the chances of fertilization.
   a. True
   b. False

6. Tracking cervical mucus may enhance the chances of fertilization.
   a. True
   b. False

7. Monitoring basal body temperature may enhance the chances of fertilization.
   a. True
   b. False

8. Which of the following is a NOT a cause of male infertility?
   a. Mutated sperm
   b. Autoimmune disease
   c. Congenital disorders
   d. Pituitary abnormality
   e. None of the above

9. Checking blood samples for estrogen levels in females may enhance the chances of fertilization.
   a. True
   b. False

10. The ovaries failure to ovulate may cause infertility in females.
    a. True
    b. False

11. Michael and Taylor are trying to have a baby. They found out that Michael has a very low sperm count. What fertility method would be the primary candidate?
    a. Adoption
    b. In vitro fertilization
    c. Artificial insemination
    d. Embryonic transfer
    e. None of the above

12. What is the major factor for infertility in women?
    a. Age
    b. Drug abuse
    c. Anovulation
    d. Menopause
    e. All of the above

13. Men do not experience age-related infertility.
    a. True
    b. False

14. Which of the following STI's can cause a woman to be infertile?
    a. HIV
    b. HPV
    c. HSV
    d. PID
    e. All of the above

15. A woman over the age of 35 years of age is considered infertile after one month of trying to conceive.
    a. True
    b. False

16. In vitro fertilization is a cheap procedure for infertile couples.
    a. True
    b. False

FREE RESPONSE

1. Describe several causes of infertility in men.

_____

_____

_____

_____

2. Describe several causes of infertility in women.

_____

_____

_____

_____

3. What is ART?

_____

_____

_____

_____

4. Compare and contrast ZIFT and GIFT.

_____

_____

_____

_____

5. Discuss the procedure for In Vitro Fertilization.

_____

_____

_____

_____

6. What are the pros and cons of egg donation?

_____

_____

_____

_____

7. List the benefits of adoption.

_____

_____

_____

_____

8. Discuss the ethical issues of cloning.

_____

_____

_____

_____

CHAPTER 13.

SEXUALLY TRANSMITTED DISEASES

Section 1

Match each term with the appropriate definition.

1. Candidiasis
2. Chlamydia
3. Gummas
4. Hepatitis B
5. Herpes simplex virus
6. Human immunodeficiency virus
7. Human papilloma virus
8. Lymphogranuloma venereum
9. Pediculosis pubis
10. Reiter's syndrome
11. Scabies
12. Syphillis
13. Trichomoniasis
14. Venereal diseases

a. Antibiotics is the primary form of treatment
b. Arthritis triggered by an infection
c. Cause genital warts
d. Crabs
e. Fungal infection
f. Infection of the lymphatic system caused by Chlamydia
g. Infection that results in AIDS
h. Mite infestation
i. Non-cancerous growths caused by syphilis
j. Protozoal infection
k. Sexually transmitted diseases
l. Symptoms include chancre
m. Symptoms include cold sores
n. Viral infection that attacks the liver

Section 2

Match each term with the appropriate structure.

1. Cervicitis
2. Cystitis
3. Endometritis
4. Orchitis
5. Proctitis
6. Salpingitis
7. Urethritis
8. Vaginitis
9. Vulvitis

a. Anus
b. Bladder
c. Cervix
d. Oviduct
e. Testes
f. Urethra
g. Uterus
h. Vagina
i. Vulva

Section 3

Match each term with the appropriate definition.

1. AZT
2. Chancroid
3. Cytotoxic T cell
4. Edema
5. Enfuvirtide
6. Erythema
7. Helper T cell
8. Molluscum contagiosum
9. Penicillin
10. Pruritus

a. Antibiotic
b. Antiretroviral medication
c. HIV fusion inhibitor
d. Itching
e. Redness
f. Soldier cells of the immune system
g. Swelling
h. T cells that are infected by HIV
i. Ulceration of the lymph nodes in the groin
j. Viral skin infection

MULTIPLE CHOICE

1. Which of the following diseases is difficult to treat due to having symptoms that are asymptomatic?
   a. Chlamydia
   b. Genital herpes
   c. Syphilis
   d. All of the above

2. How can someone become infected with an STI?
   a. Vaginal sex
   b. Anal sex
   c. Oral sex
   d. Skin to skin
   e. All of the above

3. Which of the following STI's can't be completely prevented with proper use of a condom?
   a. Gonorrhea
   b. Chlamydia
   c. Trichomoniasis
   d. Genital herpes
   e. None of the above

4. What are the signs and symptoms of Chlamydia?
   a. Itching
   b. Painful urination
   c. Vaginal discharge
   d. Testicular swelling
   e. All of the above

5. Which STD can be transmitted by damp towels?
   a. Syphilis
   b. Chlamydia
   c. Trichomoniasis
   d. Genital herpes
   e. HPV

6. Syphilis is a _____.
   a. Bacteria
   b. Virus
   c. Protozoa
   d. Fungus
   e. Parasite

7. Which STI is correlated with cervical cancer in women?
   a. Scabies
   b. Chlamydia
   c. Trichomoniasis
   d. Genital herpes
   e. HPV

8. If an STD is detected early, many can be easily treated. Which STD can't be treated?
   a. Gonorrhea
   b. Chlamydia
   c. Trichomoniasis
   d. HIV
   e. Scabies

9. Opportunistic infections are diseases that benefit from a vulnerable immune system.
   a. True
   b. False

10. Which STI is diagnosed by the presence of a single chancre?
    a. Syphilis
    b. Chlamydia
    c. Trichomoniasis
    d. Genital herpes
    e. HPV

11. Which STDs may have no symptoms?
    a. Syphilis
    b. Chlamydia
    c. Trichomoniasis
    d. Genital herpes
    e. HPV

12. What is the most common symptom for most STI's?
    a. Itching
    b. Pain
    c. Swelling
    d. Redness
    e. Asymptomatic

13. Which of the following are parasitic infections?
    a. Gonorrhea
    b. Chlamydia
    c. Trichomoniasis
    d. HIV
    e. Scabies

14. Pap smear are used to test for cervical cancer.
    a. True
    b. False

15. There is no difference between Herpes Simplex 1 and Herpes Simplex 2.
    a. True
    b. False

16. What is the most common opportunistic infection of people with AIDS?
    a. Kaposi's Sarcoma
    b. Pneumocystis carinii pneumonia
    c. Tuberculosis
    d. Wasting syndrome
    e. None of the above

17. HIV infects _____.
    a. Helper T cell
    b. Killer B cell
    c. Macrophages
    d. Helper B cells
    e. Killer T cells

18. When are HIV antibodies detectable in the blood after the first infection?
    a. 2-6 hours
    b. 2-6 days
    c. 2-6 month
    d. 2-6 years

19. Opportunistic infections are diseases that are not life threatening to people with AIDS.
    a. True
    b. False

20. Which following types of sexual interaction demonstrates the highest risk for spreading HIV among men and women?
    a. Anal intercourse
    b. Oral sex
    c. Vaginal intercourse
    d. All of the above are risky

21. What is the mechanism of anti-retroviral medication?
    a. They amplify the immune system
    b. They fight opportunistic infections
    c. They interfere with HIV replication
    d. They kill the HIV
    e. All of the above

22. Which type of testing is used to test for HIV positive blood?
    a. Western blot
    b. ELISA
    c. Northern blot
    d. Two of the above
    e. All of the above

FREE RESPONSE

1. How are STDs transferred from person to person?

_____
_____
_____
_____

2. Name a bacterial STD. What are the signs and symptoms? Provide the treatment option.

_____
_____
_____
_____

3. Name a viral STD. What are the signs and symptoms? Provide the treatment option.

_____
_____
_____
_____

4. Name a protozoal STD. What are the signs and symptoms? Provide the treatment option.

_____
_____
_____
_____

5. When treating bacterial infections, why is the specimen culture an important procedure for the final diagnosis?

_____
_____
_____
_____

6. List and describe the stages of syphilis.

_____
_____
_____
_____

7. Discuss several drugs therapy that are used to treat HIV infection and its respective mechanism of action.

_____
_____
_____
_____

Made in the USA
Columbia, SC
15 August 2019